100 Things
you should know about
Fossils

100 Things
you should know about
Fossils

Steve Parker

Consultant: Camilla de la Bedoyere

MASON CREST PUBLISHERS INC.
370 Reed Road
Broomall, Pennsylvania 19008
(866)MCP-BOOK (toll free)
www.masoncrest.com

ISBN: 978-1-4222-2000-9
Series ISBN (15 titles): 978-1-4222-1993-5

9 8 7 6 5 4 3 2

Cataloging-in-Publication Data on file with the Library of Congress.
Printed in the U.S.A.

First published in 2009 by Miles Kelly Publishing Ltd
Bardfield Centre, Great Bardfield, Essex, CM7 4SL

Editorial Director: Belinda Gallagher

Art Director: Jo Brewer

Volume Designer: Andrea Slane

Image Manager: Lorraine King

Indexer: Jane Parker

Production Manager: Elizabeth Brunwin

Reprographics: Anthony Cambray, Stephan Davis, Ian Paulyn

ACKNOWLEDGEMENTS
The publishers would like to thank the following artists
who have contributed to this book:

Mike Foster, Ian Jackson, Mike Saunders

All other artworks from the Miles Kelly Artwork Bank

The publishers would like to thank the following sources
for the use of their photographs:

Cover: Francois Gohier/Ardea

Page 6 Annie Griffiths Belt/Corbis; 8 Layne Kennedy/Corbis; 9 DK Limited; 11(t) Reuters, (b) Sinclair Stammers/Science
Photo Library; 18 Michael Amendolia/Corbis; 21 Alan Sirulnikoff/Science Photo Library; 25(t) Jaroslaw Grudzinski;
27 sciencephotos/Alamy; 28 Martin B Withers/FLPA; 29 Sheila Terry/Science Photo Library; 31 Mike Nelson/Corbis;
32 Martin Schutt/Corbis; 33(t) Paul A. Souders/Corbis, (b) NASA/GSFC/METI/ERSDAC/JAROS/Science Photo
Library; 34 Ted Soqui/Corbis; 35(t) Reuters/Corbis; 36 Michael S. Yamashita/Corbis; 37(t) Mauro Fermariello/Science
Photo Library; 38 Bill Varie/Corbis; 42 Ladislav Janicek/Zefa/Corbis; 43(t) Louie Psihoyos/Corbis, (b) Sipa Press/Rex
Features; 45(c) Bettmann/Corbis; 46(t) Pascal Goetgheluck/Science Photo Library, (b) Louie Psihoyos/Corbis

All other photographs are from:

Corel, digitalSTOCK, digitalvision, fotolia.com, iStockphoto.com, John Foxx,
PhotoAlto, PhotoDisc, PhotoEssentials, PhotoPro, Stockbyte

Contents

Recreating the past

1 **Without fossils, we would know nothing about prehistoric life.** Fossils are the remains of animals and plants that died a very long time ago and became preserved in rocks. These remains are our "window on the past." They show us the amazing variety of life that thrived and then disappeared over millions of years of Earth's history.

▲ A preserved rhinoceros skeleton gradually emerges from ten–million–year–old rocks at a fossil excavation or "dig" in Nebraska. Removing the remains is just the first part of recreating how this great beast looked, lived and died.

What are fossils?

2 Fossils are the preserved remains of once-living things, such as bones, teeth and claws. Usually the remains were buried in sediments—layers of tiny particles such as sand, silt or mud. Very slowly, the layers and the remains inside them turned into solid rock.

3 In general, it takes at least 10,000 years, but usually millions, for fossils to form. So the remains of living things that are a few hundred or thousand years old, such as the bandage-wrapped mummies of pharaohs in ancient Egypt, are not true fossils.

▲ A seed cone fossil of the extinct plant *Williamsonia*.

◄ Teeth are very hard and so make excellent fossils—especially those from *Tyrannosaurus rex!*

4 Many kinds of once-living things have formed fossils. They include all kinds of animals, from enormous whales and dinosaurs to tiny flies and beetles. There are fossils of plants too, from small mosses and flowers to immense trees. Even microscopic bacteria have been preserved.

▶ It is unusual for thin, delicate bones, such as those of the bat *Icaronycteris*, to fossilize.

5 In most cases, fossils formed from the hard parts of living things that did not rot away soon after death. As well as bones, teeth and claws, these include shells, scales and the bark, roots, cones and seeds of plants.

6 Much more rarely, soft parts have been preserved as fossils, such as flower petals and worm bodies. Where this has happened, it gives a fascinating glimpse into how these ancient life-forms looked and lived.

▼ The tube worms' soft bodies soon decayed but their hard, coiled tubes were preserved in the seabed mud.

QUIZ

Which of these are true fossils?
A. A bird called the dodo, which died out over 300 years ago
B. Two-thousand-year-old pots and vases from ancient Rome
C. The first shellfish that appeared in the sea over 500 million years ago

Answer:
C is a true fossil.
The others are much too recent.

9

Fossils in myth and legend

7 Centuries ago, the word "fossil" was used for anything dug out of the ground. This included strange-shaped rocks, crystals and gold nuggets. However, "fossil" gradually came to mean the remains of once-living plants or animals.

▲ Fossilized *Gryphea* oyster shells were known as "devil's toenails" due to their curved shape.

8 Long ago, some people regarded fossils as rocks and stones that had been specially shaped by gods to resemble animal teeth, tree bark and similar items. People believed this could be to show the gods' great powers and to test the faith of believers.

▶ It was once believed that ammonites (prehistoric sea creatures) were snakes that had turned to stone. This ammonite fossil has had a snake's head carved on it.

I DON'T BELIEVE IT!

The ancient Greeks likened ammonite fossils to coiled goat horns, believing them to be sacred because they associated them with the horned god, Jupiter Ammon.

9 In some parts of the world, fossils were seen as the remains of animals that perished in a terrible catastrophe. An example was the Great Flood as described in the Bible. A man named Noah managed to save many creatures by building an ark, but most perished in the rising waters.

◀ Bird or dinosaur? This small dinosaur was preserved with its body covering of feathers.

10 In ancient China, people once regarded fossils as the remains of dragons, giant serpents and similar monsters. Modern science shows that such animals never existed, but they seemed very real to people many years ago because they featured in tales of myth and legend.

11 Some fossils had their own myths. Rod-like fossils with pointed ends come from inside the bodies of belemnites, which were prehistoric relatives of squid. They were called "thunderstones," from the belief that they formed when lightning hit the ground.

▶ Belemnites were ancient sea creatures related to cuttlefish and octopuses. The fossilized pointed shell from inside the body is sometimes called a "belemnite bullet."

Fossils get scientific

12 **People turned to science to explain fossils.** Danish geologist (rock expert) Nicolas Steno (1638–1686) noticed that objects called "tongue stones" looked similar to the teeth of living sharks. He wondered if the teeth of ancient sharks had turned to stone.

13 **French scientist Georges Cuvier (1769–1832) showed that fossils of elephants were similar to those living today.** He suggested they had become extinct—died out forever. This caused a great stir. Most people at that time believed God created animals and plants and would never let any of them die out.

▼ Cuvier studied and named the fossil skull of the huge prehistoric sea lizard *Mosasaurus*.

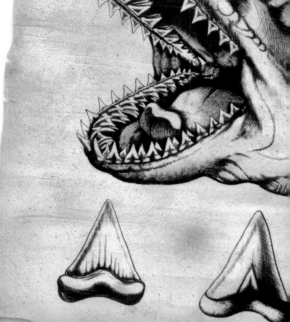

▲ Nicolas Steno made sketches of the strange, pointed "rocks" he found, and saw that they were similar in shape to the teeth of living sharks.

I DON'T BELIEVE IT!

Before scientists could explain how fossils formed, bones of huge animals such as dinosaurs were thought to be from human giants—some more than 16 feet (5 meters) tall!

14 In the 1820s, English doctor Gideon Mantell (1790–1852) found some huge fossil teeth similar to those of the iguana lizard, but bigger. He called the beast they came from *Iguanodon*. This was the first dinosaur to be named. Soon the search was on for fossils of more dinosaurs and other extinct animals.

15 In 1859, English naturalist Charles Darwin (1809–1882) published his book *On The Origin of Species*. In it, Darwin suggested that species (kinds) of living things that could not succeed in the struggle for survival died out or changed into new kinds, leaving fossils on the way.

16 During the 1800s, paleontology became a new and important branch of science. This is the study of prehistoric life and it relies greatly on fossils of all kinds.

◄ Darwin examined fossils of the giant sloth *Megatherium* and wrote: "Existing animals have a close relation in form to extinct species."

How fossils form

▼ All living things die. Those living in water, such as this ichthyosaur, are more likely to leave fossils than those on land.

17 When a living thing dies, its flesh and other soft parts start to rot. Sometimes they are eaten by scavenging creatures such as worms and insects. The harder parts, such as teeth and bones, rot more slowly and last longer.

18 Fossil formation usually begins like this, and very often in water. Sediments tend to settle on dead animals and plants in ponds, lakes, rivers and seas. This is the main reason why most fossils are of plants and animals that lived in water or somehow got washed into water.

1. After death, the ichthyosaur sinks to the seabed. Worms, crabs and other scavengers eat its soft body parts.

20

Water trickles into the sediments and once-living remains. The water contains dissolved substances such as minerals and salts. Gradually, these replace the once-living parts and turn them and the sediments into solid rock. This is called permineralization.

21

Most living things rot away soon after death, so the chances of anything becoming a fossil are slim. Also, sedimentary rock layers change over time, becoming heated and bent, which can destroy fossils in them. The chances of anyone finding a fossil are even tinier. This is why the record of fossils in rocks represents only a tiny proportion of prehistoric life.

19

Over time, more sediment layers settle on top of the remains. As they are covered deeper, further rotting or scavenging is less likely.

2. Sediments cover the hard body parts, such as bones and teeth, which gradually turn into solid rock.

3. Millions of years later, the upper rock layers wear away and the fossil remains are exposed.

Mold and cast fossils

22 Because of the way fossils form, they are almost always found in sedimentary rocks such as sandstone, limestone, chalk, shale and slate. Other kinds of rocks, such as igneous rocks that cool from red-hot, runny lava erupted from volcanoes, do not contain fossils.

▼ Ammonites were fierce hunting animals related to squid. They died out with the dinosaurs 65 million years ago.

Cast fossil

Mold fossil

▲ This ammonite fossil has split into part and counterpart, with a mold and cast fossil inside.

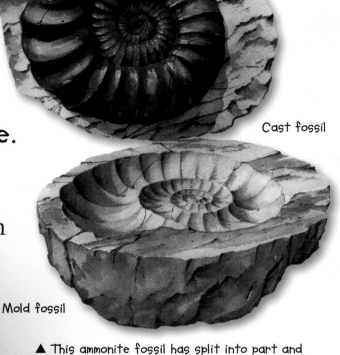

23 As the bits and pieces of sediments become solid rock, the once-living remains within them may not. They are dissolved by water and gradually washed away. The result is a hole in the rock the same shape as the remains, called a mold fossil.

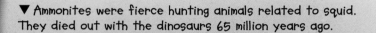

24 After more time, the hole or mold in the rock may fill with minerals deposited by water. This produces a lump of stone that is different in make-up from the surrounding rocks, but is the same shape as the original remains. This is known as a cast fossil.

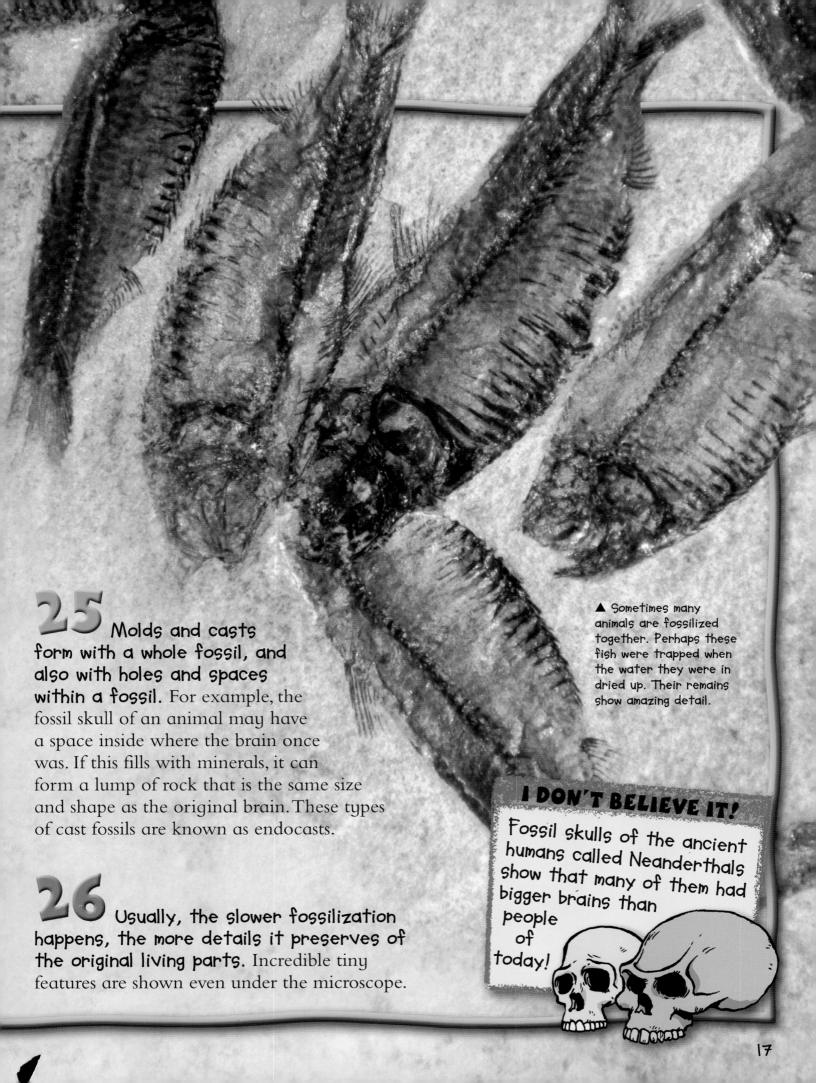

25 Molds and casts form with a whole fossil, and also with holes and spaces within a fossil. For example, the fossil skull of an animal may have a space inside where the brain once was. If this fills with minerals, it can form a lump of rock that is the same size and shape as the original brain. These types of cast fossils are known as endocasts.

26 Usually, the slower fossilization happens, the more details it preserves of the original living parts. Incredible tiny features are shown even under the microscope.

▲ Sometimes many animals are fossilized together. Perhaps these fish were trapped when the water they were in dried up. Their remains show amazing detail.

I DON'T BELIEVE IT!

Fossil skulls of the ancient humans called Neanderthals show that many of them had bigger brains than people of today!

Special preservation

▲ This frog dried out before its flesh could rot away, leaving its mummified remains.

27 Once-living things can be preserved in many different ways. Mummification is when a dead plant or animal is left to dry out slowly. Some dinosaurs and animals have been preserved in this way in the windblown sands of deserts.

28 Amber is the sap (sticky resin) from prehistoric trees, especially conifers, that has been fossilized. If small creatures became trapped by the resin, they are preserved within it. Insects, spiders, frogs, and even leaves and seeds have all been preserved in this way.

◄ Amber preserves amazingly small details, even the delicate wings of this fly.

29

Natural pools of thick, sticky tar ooze up from the ground in some places such as forests and scrubland. Animals that become trapped sink into the tar pit and may be preserved—even huge creatures, such as wolves, deer, bears, saber-tooth cats and mammoths.

► In 1977, the perfectly preserved body of this baby mammoth was found thawing out in Siberia. The mammoth had been trapped in ice for thousands of years.

30

Being naturally frozen into the ice of the far north or south is a type of preservation. It's not true fossilization, but as the ice melts it reveals deep-frozen flowers, trees, mammoths and deer.

◄ Fossilized human footprints in southeastern Australia. The spacing of fossil footprints, called trackways, show how their makers walked and ran.

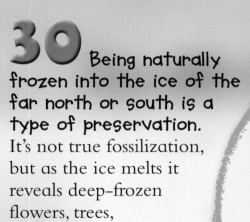

MATCH-UP!

Match the following with how they were preserved.
A. Desert-living dinosaur
B. Wolf in woodland
C. Tree-dwelling insect

1 Natural tar pit
2 Trapped in amber
3 Mummification.

Answers:
A3 B1 C2

31

Trace fossils are not actual body parts of once-living things. They are signs or "traces" made by them, which then became fossilized. Examples include the footprints of animals, their burrows, egg shells, teeth marks and scratch marks, which can all turn to stone.

32 Some rare and exciting fossils were not formed from the hard parts of living things. They were once soft creatures such as worms, jellyfish and anemones, preserved in unusual conditions.

33 Almost all living things need oxygen to survive. In some kinds of seabed mud, the water is still and brings no oxygen, so there is no life. If sea animals and plants end up here, maybe after an underwater mudslide, there are no living things to rot them in the usual way.

34 In oxygen–less conditions, dead, soft-bodied creatures and plants gradually undergo a strange type of fossilization into carbon films and impressions. These are like smears of oil or powder in the rock. They occur especially in sedimentary rocks called shales or mudstones.

◀ Jellyfish are soft and floppy, but they have on rare occasions left fossilized impressions in sand and mud.

◄ This fossil, called *Mawsonites*, may have been a jellyfish, the root-like holdfast of a seaweed or an animal's burrow network in the mud.

35

About 505 million years ago some seabed mud slid and slumped into deep, oxygen-free water. The black shale rocks that formed are at Burgess Pass in the Rocky Mountains of British Columbia, Canada.

36

Burgess Shale fossils number many tens of thousands. They include the strangest kinds of creatures, resembling worms, jellyfish and shrimps. Some are like no other animals ever known.

▼ The Burgess Shale area is a World Heritage Site. It has yielded more than 60,000 fossils from the Cambrian Period, 582—488 million years ago.

37

Rare fossils give a tiny glimpse into the myriad creatures that thrived long ago, but are rarely preserved. They show that of all the kinds of animals and plants that have ever lived, more than 999 out of 1,000 are long gone and extinct (died out).

Fossils and time

38 **Fossils are studied by many kinds of scientists.** Paleontologists are general experts on fossils and prehistoric life. Paleozoologists specialize in prehistoric creatures, and paleobotanists in prehistoric plants. Geologists study rocks, soil and other substances that make up the Earth. All of these sciences allow us to work out the immense prehistory of the Earth.

39 **Earth's existence is divided into enormous lengths of time called eons, which are split into eras, then periods, epochs and finally, stages.** Each of these time divisions is marked by changes in the rocks formed at the time—and if the rocks are sedimentary, by the fossils they contain. The whole time span, from the formation of the Earth 4,600 million years ago to today, is known as the geological time scale.

▼ Starting with the Cambrian Period (far right), this timeline shows 11 major time periods in Earth's history. It gives examples of some of the fossil animals and plants that have been found for each period. 'MYA' stands for 'millions of years ago'.

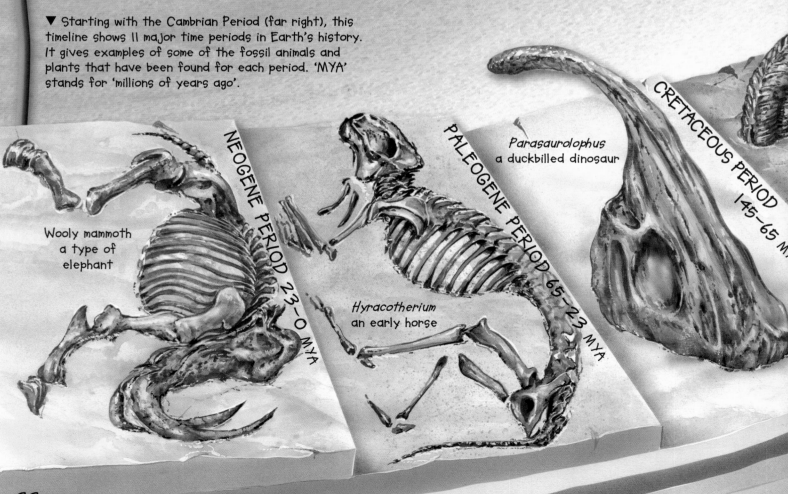

Wooly mammoth a type of elephant

NEOGENE PERIOD 23–0 MYA

Hyracotherium an early horse

PALEOGENE PERIOD 65–23 MYA

Parasaurolophus a duckbilled dinosaur

CRETACEOUS PERIOD 145–65 MYA

CAMBRIAN PERIOD
542–488 MYA

Trilobite
a shelled marine creature

ORDOVICIAN PERIOD
488–444 MYA

SILURIAN PERIOD 444–416 MYA

Graptolite
a simple marine animal

Birkenia
a type of fish

Crinoid
a simple marine animal

DEVONIAN PERIOD 416–359 MYA

CARBONIFEROUS PERIOD 359–299 MYA

40 An example of a geological time division is the Cretaceous Period, from 145 to 65 million years ago. It is named after creta or *kreta*, a Latin word for chalk. Due to temperature, rainfall and other climate conditions, layers of chalk rocks formed. They contained fossils such as certain kinds of shellfish, the winged reptiles known as pterosaurs and many kinds of dinosaurs.

PERMIAN PERIOD 299–251 MYA

Lepidodendron
a primitive tree

TRIASSIC PERIOD 251–200 MYA

JURASSIC PERIOD 200–145 MYA

Diplocaulus
an early amphibian

Rhamphorhynchus
a winged reptile

Stephanoceras
a type of ammonite

MAKE CHALK FOSSILS

You will need:
chalk sticks   metal teaspoon

Chalk often contains fossil shellfish. Find pictures of long, thin examples, such as razorshells, mussels and belemnites. Use the spoon to scrape and carve the chalk sticks into shapes to make your own "fossil" museum.

Working out dates

41 **"Dating" a fossil means finding out how old it is.** Usually, rocks found deeper in the ground are older than the rock layers above them, so any fossils they contain are also older. Sedimentary rock layers and their fossils have been compared to build up a picture of which fossilized plants and animals lived when.

▼ Different rock layers can be clearly seen in the Grand Canyon. The layers have been revealed by the Colorado River as it winds its way through the canyon.

42 **If a new fossil is found, it can be compared with this overall pattern to get an idea of its age.** This is known as relative dating—finding the date of a fossil relative to other fossils of known ages.

▲ Some types of chalk rocks are almost entirely made of the fossils of small sea creatures.

43 Certain types of plants and animals were very common, survived for millions of years and left plenty of fossil remains. This makes them extremely useful for relative dating. They are known as marker, index, indicator, guide or zone fossils.

44 Most index fossils come from the sea, where preservation is more likely than on land. They include multi-legged trilobites, curly-shelled ammonites, ball-shaped echinoids (sea urchins) and net-like graptolites. On land, tough pollen grains and spores from plants are useful index fossils.

Magnetic field

N

S

▲ Earth's magnetism has changed and even reversed over millions of years, helping to date fossils.

▶ Trilobites make good index fossils. Different kinds appeared and then died out between 530 million and about 250 million years ago.

45 Earth's natural magnetic field changed many times through prehistory. When some kinds of igneous rocks formed by cooling, the magnetism was "frozen" into them, known as paleomagnetism. It can be dated by comparison with the whole pattern of magnetic changes through Earth's history.

How many years ago?

46 Relative dating, by comparing fossils with each other, shows if one fossil is older or younger than another. But how do we know the actual age of fossils in millions of years, known as absolute dating?

47 The main kind of absolute dating is based on naturally occurring substances that give off tiny amounts of rays and particles, known as radioactivity. As they give off these weak forms of energy, the substances —known as radioisotopes—change or "decay" slightly. The amounts of different radioisotopes in a fossil can be measured to show how long ago it formed. This is known as radiometric dating.

48 Several kinds of substances are used for radiometric dating. Each decays at a set rate, some slower than others. Very slow ones are useful for the oldest fossils, and the fastest ones for young fossils.

◀ The rocks of the Canadian Shield, a huge area of land in eastern and central Canada, have been dated to more than 2,500 million years ago.

49 **Radiocarbon dating is based on the change or decay of one form of carbon known as C14.** It happens relatively fast and is useful for a time span up to 60,000 years ago. This helps with dating young fossils and with items such as deep-frozen mammoths.

50 **In potassium-argon dating, the element potassium changes into argon very slowly, over billions of years.** It's useful for rock layers formed just above or below fossils from billions of years ago to about 100,000 years ago. Rubidium-strontium and uranium-lead dating can reveal the age of even older rocks, almost back to when Earth began.

▼ Geologists measure tiny amounts of radioactivity in rocks and fossils using equipment such as Geiger counters.

▼ Radiocarbon dating.

1. Wooly mammoth eats plants containing C14

2. Mammoth dies, no more C14 is taken in

3. Half of C14 decays every 5,730 years

Fossil-hunting takes off

51 From the early 19th century, fossil-hunting became more popular. Towns and cities, as well as rich individuals, began to establish museums and collections of the "wonders of nature," with displays of stuffed animals, pinned insects, pressed flowers—and lots of fossils.

52 People began to earn a living by finding and selling fossils. One of the first was Mary Anning (1799–1847) of Lyme Regis, southern England. For many years she collected fossils from the seashore, where waves and storms regularly cracked open boulders and cliffs to reveal new finds. Mary discovered fossil fish, ichthyosaurs, plesiosaurs, pterosaurs and many other animals.

▶ As in Mary Anning's time, fossils still appear from the rocks at Lyme Regis.

FOSSIL MATCH

Match the scientific names of these fossils with the places they were found.
A. Argentinosaurus (dinosaur)
B. Toxorhynchites mexicanus (mosquito in amber)
C. Proconsul africanus (ape-monkey)

1 Mexico, Central America
2 Argentina, South America
3 Africa

Answers:
A2 B1 C3

53 In 1881, the British Museum opened its display of natural history collections in London, which showed fossils and similar wonders from around the world. Other great cities had similar museums and sent fossil-hunters to remote places for the most spectacular finds.

▲ By the 1860s many museums had fossils on display, such as this "sea serpent" or mosasaur.

▼ Cope and Marsh found and described about 130 new kinds of dinosaurs.

Othniel Charles Marsh

Edward Drinker Cope

54 Between the 1870s and 1890s, two of the leading fossil-hunters were Americans Othniel Charles Marsh and Edward Drinker Cope. Their teams tried to outdo each other to discover the most and best fossil dinosaurs, as well as other animals and plants too.

▲ The first fossil stegosaur skulls were found in the 1870s.

▶ The dinosaur *Stegosaurus* was named by Marsh in 1877.

55 From the early 1900s, fossil-hunting spread to Africa, and then in the 1920s, to Mongolia and China. From the 1970s, there were finds in South America and Australia. Today, fossil-hunters go all over the world in search of new discoveries.

Famous hot spots

56 Some places around the world have become famous for their fossils. These places are often in the news because of dinosaur remains. However, dinosaur finds are only some of the thousands of fossils being unearthed and studied.

▼ This map shows some of the most famous fossil sites around the world.

57 The Midwest "Badlands" of North America has many famous fossil sites. At Dinosaur National Monument, on the border between Colorado and Utah, the rocks date to almost 150 million years ago. Apart from dinosaur remains, they also yield fossils of crocodiles, turtles, frogs, shellfish and plants.

USA
Dinosaur National Monument

◄ Dinosaur fossils at Dinosaur National Monument. This park opened in 1915 and receives over 350,000 visitors each year.

BRAZIL
Santana Formation

58 In northeast Brazil in South America, there are limestone rocks about 110–90 million years old known as the Santana Formation. Detailed fossils include pterosaurs, reptiles, frogs, insects and plants. Some fossil fish were preserved with the remains of their last meals inside their bodies.

◄ This 100-million-year-old dragonfly is one of thousands from Brazil's Santana Formation rocks.

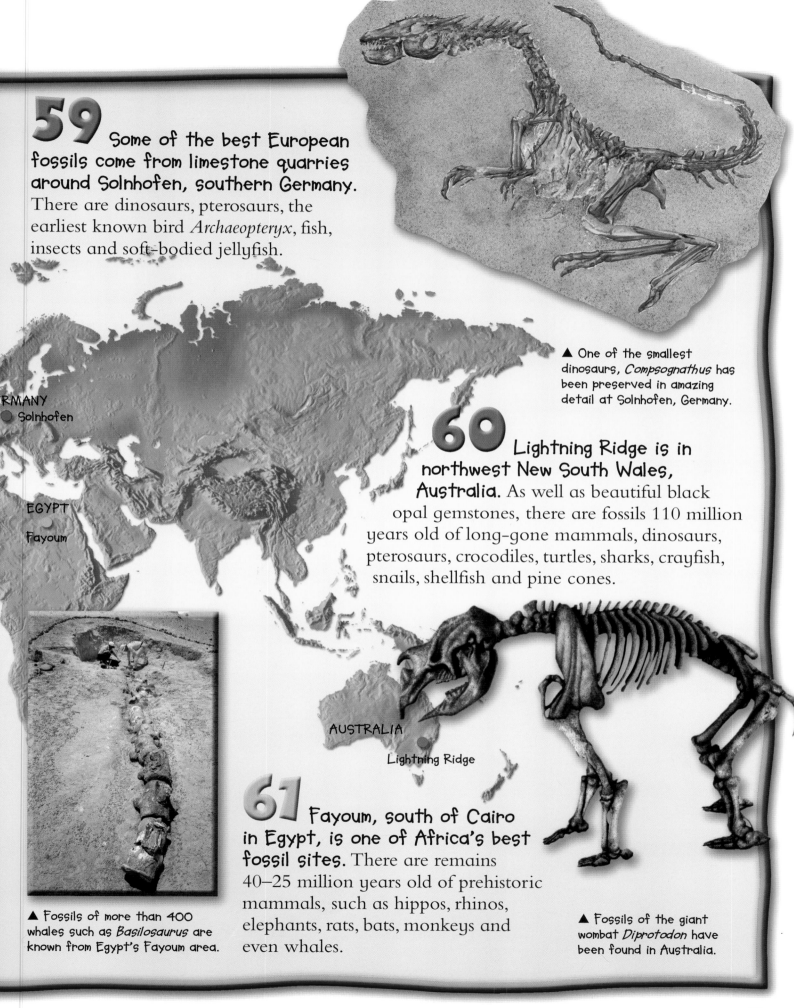

59 Some of the best European fossils come from limestone quarries around Solnhofen, southern Germany. There are dinosaurs, pterosaurs, the earliest known bird *Archaeopteryx*, fish, insects and soft-bodied jellyfish.

GERMANY
Solnhofen

EGYPT
Fayoum

▲ One of the smallest dinosaurs, *Compsognathus* has been preserved in amazing detail at Solnhofen, Germany.

60 Lightning Ridge is in northwest New South Wales, Australia. As well as beautiful black opal gemstones, there are fossils 110 million years old of long-gone mammals, dinosaurs, pterosaurs, crocodiles, turtles, sharks, crayfish, snails, shellfish and pine cones.

AUSTRALIA
Lightning Ridge

61 Fayoum, south of Cairo in Egypt, is one of Africa's best fossil sites. There are remains 40–25 million years old of prehistoric mammals, such as hippos, rhinos, elephants, rats, bats, monkeys and even whales.

▲ Fossils of more than 400 whales such as *Basilosaurus* are known from Egypt's Fayoum area.

▲ Fossils of the giant wombat *Diprotodon* have been found in Australia.

Looking for fossils

62 **Where do we find fossils?**
Fossil-hunters use many kinds of
aids and clues to find the best sites.
Geological maps show which
kinds of rocks are found at or just
under the surface. To contain
fossils, these rocks need to be
sedimentary, such as limestone.

PLAN A FOSSIL DIG

You will need:
pencil and notebook
pictures of fossil dig sites

You're in charge of a fossil-finding
trip to a remote desert. Make a
list of the equipment and supplies
you think you'll need. Look
through the pages of this book for
clues. Once you have a list, draw
a plan of your dig and decide
who to take with you.

63 **Fossil-hunters are careful to get permission
to search a site.** The landowner, land manager and local
authorities must all agree on the search methods and the
ownership of any finds. This avoids problems such as
trespassing, criminal damage and "fossil-rustling" (stealing).

▶ Paleontologists sift through rocks
and common fossils for signs of important
specimens at Bromacker Quarry, Germany.

► Year after year, sun, wind, rain and ice wear away rocks and reveal fossils at Dinosaur Provincial Park, Alberta, Canada.

64 **Good places to look for fossils are where rocks are regularly broken apart and worn away by waves, wind, sun, ice and other weather.** This is the process of erosion. It happens at cliffs, seashores, river banks and valleys, canyons and caves. It also happens where people dig quarries, mines, road and railway cuttings and building foundations.

65 **Satellite images, aerial photographs, survey trips by plane, or even just walking around show the nature of the ground.** Bare rocky areas are best, rather than areas covered with soil, plants and trees.

► This satellite photo of East Africa's Olduvai Gorge shows one of the world's best areas for prehistoric human fossils.

66 **Fossil-hunters also follow a collector's code of guidelines.** These show how to cause the least damage when digging, how to stay safe and how to restore the site afterward.

At the dig

67 Some people look for fossils in their spare time and if they find one it's a bonus. At an important site, scientists such as paleontologists organize an excavation or "dig" that can last for many months.

68 The dig area is divided into squares called a grid, usually by string or strips of wood. This is used to record the positions of the finds. As the excavation continues, the workers make notes, take photographs, draw sketches and use many other recording methods.

▼ Paleontologists dig up fossilized mammoth remains in California. The valuable specimens are wrapped in layers of sacking and plaster before being moved.

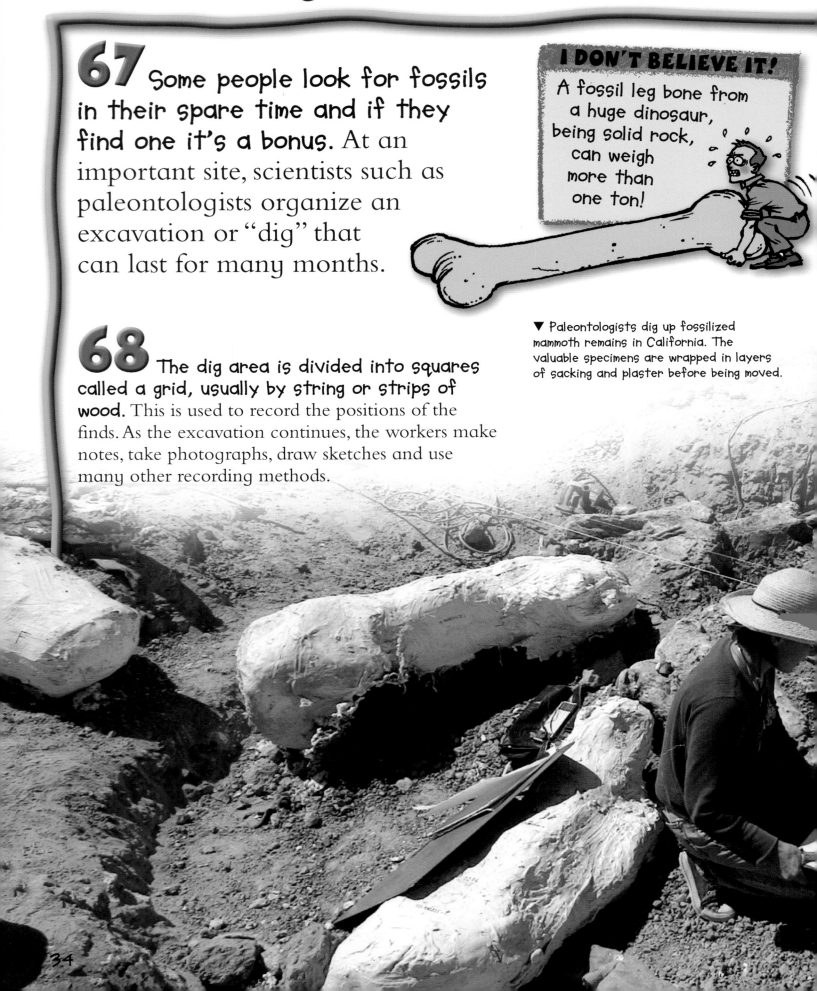

69 At first, there may be lots of loose rocks, boulders or soil to remove, called overburden. Big, powerful tools might be used, such as mechanical diggers, road drills (jackhammers) or even dynamite!

▲ It can take weeks to clean a large fossil such as this elephant skull and tusk.

70 As fossils are exposed, experts decide whether they are worth digging out. Gradually, the excavation methods become more careful, using hammers, chisels, small picks and brushes to avoid damaging the find. It can be a lengthy, difficult task. The dig site might be a baking desert, tropical swamp or freezing mountainside.

71 Small bits of loose rock might be strained to find tiny fossils. Soft, fragile fossils can be covered with material such as plaster or fiberglass, which hardens into a protective jacket. This allows the fossil to be lifted out.

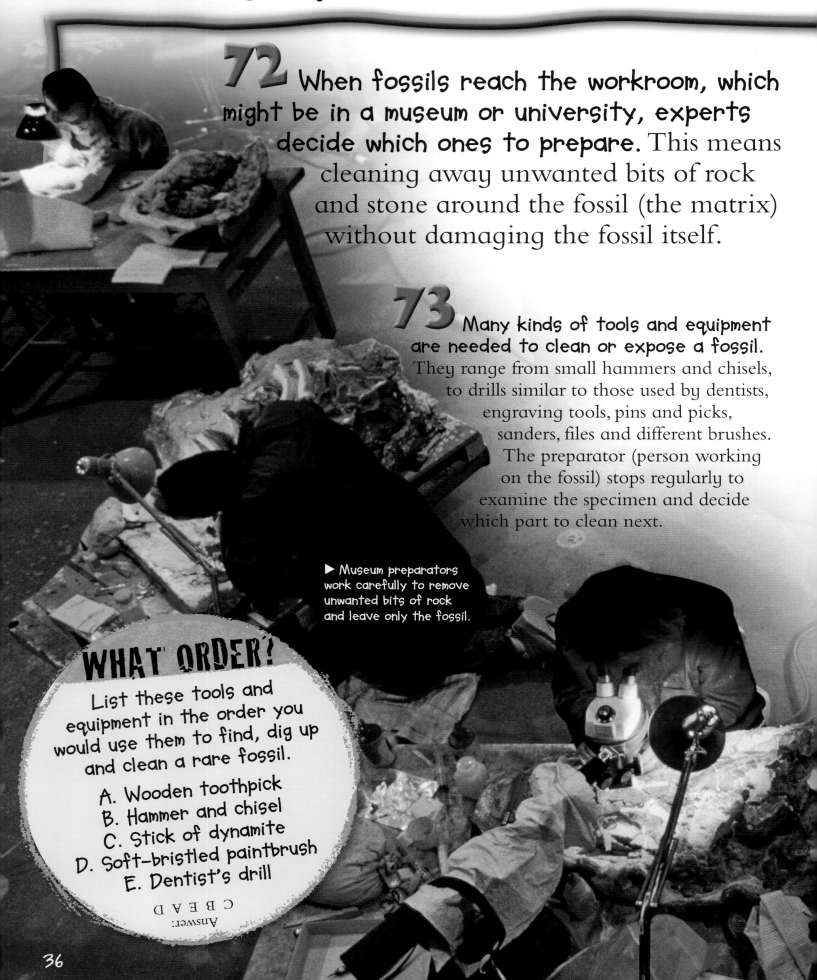

Cleaning up fossils

72 When fossils reach the workroom, which might be in a museum or university, experts decide which ones to prepare. This means cleaning away unwanted bits of rock and stone around the fossil (the matrix) without damaging the fossil itself.

73 Many kinds of tools and equipment are needed to clean or expose a fossil. They range from small hammers and chisels, to drills similar to those used by dentists, engraving tools, pins and picks, sanders, files and different brushes. The preparator (person working on the fossil) stops regularly to examine the specimen and decide which part to clean next.

▶ Museum preparators work carefully to remove unwanted bits of rock and leave only the fossil.

WHAT ORDER?

List these tools and equipment in the order you would use them to find, dig up and clean a rare fossil.

A. Wooden toothpick
B. Hammer and chisel
C. Stick of dynamite
D. Soft-bristled paintbrush
E. Dentist's drill

Answer:
C B E A D

74 Microscopes are often used to show tiny details of a fossil during preparation. Usually this is a stereoscopic microscope with two eyepieces, like binoculars, mounted on a stand with the specimen beneath.

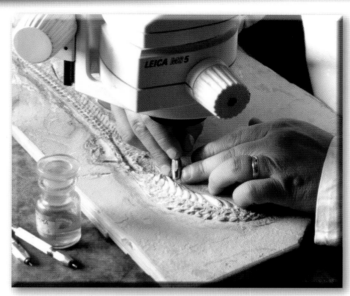

▲ The enlarged view through a stereo microscope shows lots of detail, to avoid scratching or chipping the specimen.

▶ It may take a year to dissolve rock with acid and expose the fossils —these are unhatched dinosaur eggs.

Dinosaur embryo

75 When the fossil is one type of rock and the matrix is another, preparators may use chemicals to expose the fossil. Different acids are tested on small parts of the matrix and fossil, to see if they dissolve the former but not the latter.

76 Very few animals or plants die neatly in one piece and are preserved whole. So it's incredibly rare to find a whole fossilized plant or animal with all the parts positioned as they were in life. Most fossils are bits and pieces that are crushed and distorted. Putting them back together is very difficult!

On display

77 **In a well-organized fossil collection, specimens are given catalog numbers showing where and when they were found.** They are studied, described and identified, and logged into a computer database or card index. Then the specimen can be easily recognized.

78 **Usually only exceptional fossils are chosen to display in museums, galleries and exhibitions.** They might be very large for their kind, preserved in great detail, be extremely rare, found by a famous fossil-hunter, or simply very beautiful.

79 **Fossil displays vary hugely.** Some are shelves or cabinets with simple labels. Others have fossils and reconstructions of the original animals or plants, set into a realistic scene. They may have special lighting, descriptions and diagrams, and even push-button video shows.

▼ London's Natural History Museum has some of the world's best fossil displays, such as these dinosaurs.

I DON'T BELIEVE IT!

In 2002, experts re-examined the fossil jaws of a tiny creature called *Rhyniognatha* found in 1919. They realized it was probably the earliest known insect, and that it was almost 400 million years old.

80 **Some fossils are so rare, delicate or valuable that they are not displayed—copies are.** Copies or replicas of very rare fossils might be sent to other museums so more people can study them.

81 **Copies are used for big creatures such as dinosaurs, whales and mammoths.** The original fossils are solid rock and can weigh many tons. Lightweight copies are easier and safer to put on a frame or hang by wires, to build up the animal in a lifelike position.

Fossils come alive!

82 One of the most exciting parts of fossil study is to reconstruct (rebuild) the original plant or animal. This needs a detailed knowledge of anatomy, or body structure. For example, fossils of prehistoric birds are compared to the same body parts of similar birds alive today. This is called comparative anatomy.

83 Tiny marks or "scars" on fossil bones show where the animal's muscles attached in real life. These help to reveal muscle shapes and arrangements so experts can gradually put the flesh on the (fossil) bones.

Fossil bones
Faint scars on fossil bones can help scientists work out how and where muscles were attached

▲ This reconstruction of an ankylosaur, an armored dinosaur, is being done head-first. The tail is still bare fossils of the bones.

84 We can see how a living creature walks, runs and jumps using the joints between its bones. If fossil bones have their joints preserved, their detailed shapes and designs show the range of motion and how the animal moved.

MULTI-COLORED BIRD

You will need:
pictures of *Archaeopteryx* colored pens
tracing paper   white paper

No one knows what color the first bird *Archaeopteryx* was. Look at pictures of it in books and on websites. See how its feather colors and patterns differ. Trace an outline of *Archaeopteryx* from a book and color it to your own amazing design.

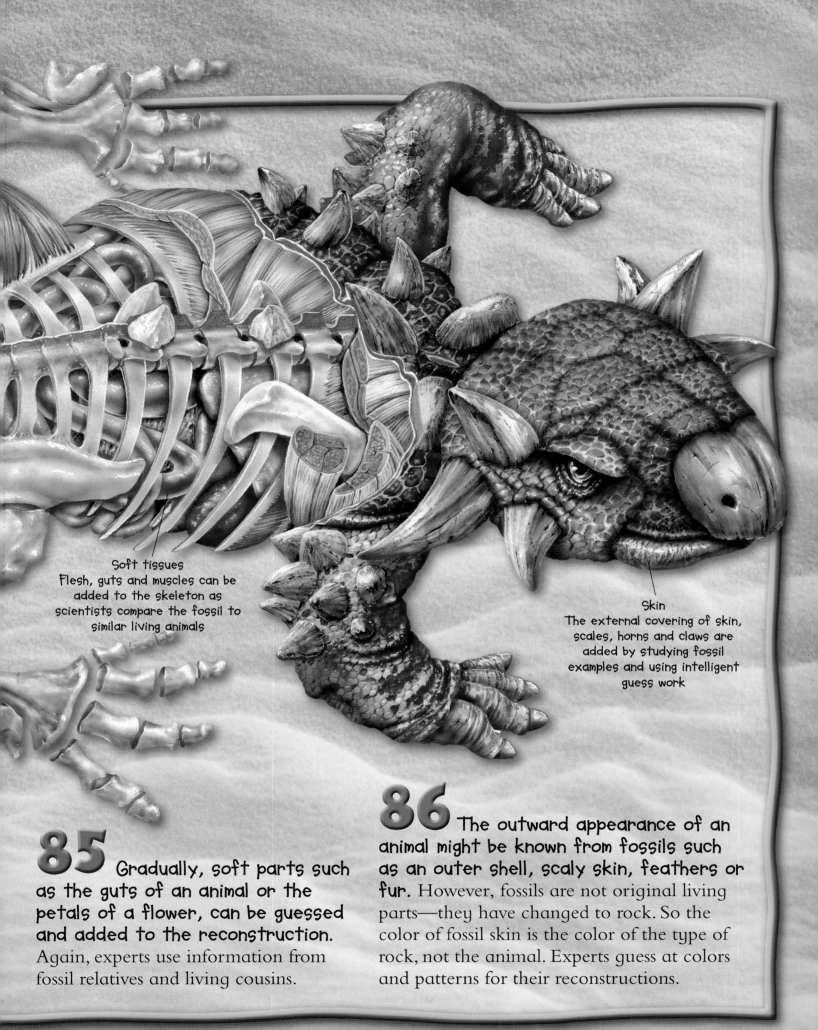

Soft tissues
Flesh, guts and muscles can be
added to the skeleton as
scientists compare the fossil to
similar living animals

Skin
The external covering of skin,
scales, horns and claws are
added by studying fossil
examples and using intelligent
guess work

85 Gradually, soft parts such as the guts of an animal or the petals of a flower, can be guessed and added to the reconstruction. Again, experts use information from fossil relatives and living cousins.

86 The outward appearance of an animal might be known from fossils such as an outer shell, scaly skin, feathers or fur. However, fossils are not original living parts—they have changed to rock. So the color of fossil skin is the color of the type of rock, not the animal. Experts guess at colors and patterns for their reconstructions.

Trading, stealing, faking

87 **Fossils are big business.** Thousands of people work at digs, in workrooms and in museums, exhibitions and galleries. A find such as a new dinosaur can hit the news headlines and make the discoverer famous— and rich!

88 **The biggest, most complete fossil *Tyrannosaurus rex* was found in 1990 near Faith, Dakota, by Sue Hendrickson.** The dinosaur was nicknamed "Sue" and there was a long legal dispute about who owned it. Finally, it was sold to the Field Museum of Chicago for more than seven million dollars!

◄ Street traders offer fossils for sale in North Africa. There is no guarantee the fossils came from the local area.

▶ Chinese paleontologist Dong Zhiming with some smuggled dinosaur eggs. Every year, police, customs and security staff uncover illegal collections such as this.

89 Real fossils, replicas and models are sold around the world by museums, shops, mail-order catalogs and on the Internet. Buyers range from leading museums to individuals who like the idea of a home fossil collection without the trouble of digging them up.

▼ Rare or unusual fossils, such as this ammonite shell showing detailed internal structure, can fetch huge sums of money at auction.

90 Stealing and faking fossils has been going on for centuries. In 1999, scientists announced a fossil creature called *Archaeoraptor* that seemed to be part-bird and part-dinosaur. *Archaeoraptor* showed how small meat-eating dinosaurs evolved into birds. However, further study revealed that the specimen was indeed part-dinosaur and part-bird, because it was a fake with separate fossils cleverly glued together.

Famous fossils

91 Many fossils and prehistoric sites around the world are massive attractions, visited by millions of people. The Petrified Forest National Park in Arizona has hundreds of huge fossilized trees and smaller specimens of animals such as dinosaurs, dating from about 225 million years ago. It receives more than half a million visitors yearly.

▲ The coelacanth is known as a "living fossil," meaning it is very similar to its long-extinct relatives.

92 The coelacanth fish was known only from fossils and thought to have been extinct for more than 60 million years. In 1938, a living coelacanth was caught off southeast Africa and more have been discovered since. Living things that are very similar to their prehistoric relatives are known as "living fossils."

▶ Thousands of fossil tree trunks and branches litter the ground at Arizona's Petrified Forest National Park.

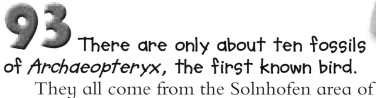

93 There are only about ten fossils of *Archaeopteryx*, the first known bird. They all come from the Solnhofen area of southern Germany. They are amazingly detailed and almost priceless.

▶ Each specimen of *Archaeopteryx* is closely guarded.

94 "Lucy" is a fossilized part-skeleton from a very early human-type creature. It was discovered in 1974 in Ethiopia, Africa and dates back about 3.2 million years. Thousands of people flock to see "her" every year.

◀ Piltdown Man was really the skull of a human from about 500 years ago combined with the jawbone of an orangutan.

I DON'T BELIEVE IT!
Animal droppings can become fossils known as coprolites. Leftovers in them can show what an animal ate. Luckily they are no longer squishy and smelly, but have become solid rock.

95 Piltdown Man is perhaps the most famous fossil fake. It was found in southeast England in 1912 and thought to be an early kind of human. In 1953 it was exposed as a hoax by new scientific methods.

Looking to the future

96 As fossil-hunting goes on around the world, scientific methods and equipment become more powerful every year. Ground-penetrating radar, X-rays and CT (computerized tomography) scanners can "see" fossils inside solid rock.

▲ A CT scanner examines the fossil skull of an ancient type of otter.

97 As we improve ways to study fossils, old specimens are looked at again to see new details. The dinosaur *Oviraptor* or "egg thief" was named because one of its fossils suggested it was stealing the eggs of another dinosaur. Then X-rays of similar eggs showed baby *Oviraptor*s inside. The "egg thief" fossil was probably looking after its own eggs.

◄ This *Oviraptor* may have died shielding its eggs from a predator, 75 million years ago.

98

Some amazing fossils of the 1990s–2000s are from Liaoning Province in northeast China. Dated to 130 million years ago, they show details of creatures and plants, including dinosaurs with feathers and a cat-sized mammal that preyed on baby dinosaurs.

▲ Fossils of the tiny feathered dinosaur *Microraptor* have been found in China.

99

New fossils provide more evidence for evolution, such as how fish changed gradually into land animals. *Panderichthys* was a fish-like creature from 380 million years ago. It had features such as finger-like bones developing in its fins.

100

Important fossil discoveries cause news and excitement around the world. They affect our ideas about prehistoric life, how Earth has changed through time, evolution and extinction. They can also help to fill in the details of where we came from.

NAME GAME

Match these nicknames of fossils with their scientific names.
A. "Lucy" B. "Stan" C. "Jaws"
D. "Spike"

1. Triceratops (dinosaur)
2. Megalodon (giant shark)
3. Australopithecus afarensis (early human)
4. Tyrannosaurus (dinosaur)

Answers:
A3 B4 C2 D1

▲ *Panderichthys* was about 3 feet (one meter) long. Its fossils come from Latvia in northeastern Europe.

Index